THE BOOK OF
PRIMROSES

BARBARA SHAW

TIMBER PRESS
Portland, Oregon

For my Grandchildren,
who love Devon and Primroses

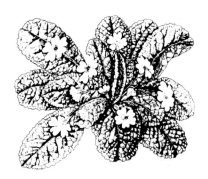

Typeset by ABM Typographics Ltd, Hull
and printed in Singapore by CS Graphics Pte Ltd
for David & Charles plc
Brunel House   Newton Abbot   Devon

First published in North America in 1991 by
Timber Press, Inc.
9999 S.W. Wilshire,
Portland, Oregon 97225, USA

ISBN 0–88192–191–2.

CONTENTS

FOREWORD

A love of primroses is almost instinctive. The very mention of the name sends the mind travelling back to April days spent searching for the first pale-yellow flowers along the hedgerows.

Though many of us may feel personal attachment towards the first flower of spring, few of us possess the talent to give visual expression to that feeling. Barbara Shaw reveals to all who turn the pages of her book the exceeding beauty of spring displayed in a simple flower. The quality of the illustrations, so sympathetic and evocative, will delight gardeners and non-practitioners alike.

Chapter 1 sets the pattern, with stories of forays along leafy Devon lanes where primroses grow so much larger and more abundantly than anywhere else. The chapter on botanical painting discloses the slow maturation process of the artist; and in this case 'botanical' means both beautiful and accurate. The author's history of primroses offers the enthusiast plenty of fresh avenues to explore, as her twenty years of research and note taking have produced some fascinating details. Having previously thought only of Clusius in the context of tulips, I must now consider him a grower of primroses as well.

Having stimulated our interest and made us reach for nursery lists and cheque book, the chapter on the cultivation of the various sorts, forms, and infinite varieties of primroses becomes essential rather than merely obligatory. Better to understand early in our infatuation that though primroses grow along copse and hedgerow in copious drifts of yellow, they are not so obliging in every garden. In my last garden, though the Asiatic species flourished, self seeding all about themselves, our native species in all forms 'miffed' and 'moped'. All that was needed was a little understanding in regard to their diet, and suddenly all temperament was exposed as merely my own ignorance.

I defy anyone to read this book, study the superb illustrations, and not love primroses more. That they will also insist on growing them is quite inevitable.

Geoffrey Smith

CHAPTER 1

MY PRIMROSE GARDEN

Primroses have enhanced my life for as long as I can remember. When I was a child growing up between the wars anybody who was housebound or needed cheering early in the year was taken a posy of primroses: it was the natural thing to do. We knew of sheltered spots in the Devon countryside where primroses would bloom in January, and always picked some for our mother to enjoy in the darker days of winter. At Easter there was a concerted effort to produce a basketful, each bunch carefully tied with wool, to decorate the church. What a joy it was on Easter morning to be greeted by that unforgettable, delicate smell of primroses and to see them, like a splash of pale sunlight at the base of the font.

So much were they associated with Devon that some of the county's paper mills sent bunches of primroses to their customers each year. Every spring during the war, when I was in the North of England, my mother sent me a shoe-box with the flowers packed in moss, nestling amid tissue paper; the memory of lifting the lid on that exquisite smell and their fragile beauty remains with me still.

Of course, in these environmentally conscious days, primrose picking would be frowned upon and quite rightly so. With far more people about, and many tourists visiting the county, if everyone picked the hedgerow flowers there would soon be none left. In the past we were taught never to pick all the flowers from one plant and always to leave a few to set seed, and, of course, none of us would have thought of digging up a wild plant. Even so, most picking was done, with special permission, on privately owned land.

With this sort of background it is hardly surprising that, when I married and had a garden of my own, some of the first things I planted were primroses. At first it was a few plants given to me by my family, then gradually I began to collect others, but space was limited and life (and the garden) was full of children and animals, including free-range pet rabbits. So it was not until we moved to our present house in 1962 that I began to collect primroses in earnest.

Our garden, set amid the hills at the southern end of the Yorkshire Dales and bordered by fields on two sides, is the perfect setting for primroses, and for all the traditional plants such as pinks, and shrub roses that blend happily with the old house and the countryside. The soil is rich, just on the acid side of neutral, and good well rotted manure is always to hand. A few trees of average height give a pleasant dappled shade, not too dense, and the land is well drained, yet reasonably moisture-retentive. In general, rainfall is high here in the hills, giving the primroses the conditions they enjoy.

I remember the sheer delight upon planting my first double white primrose, *Primula vulgaris alba plena* – still my favourite double, with its classic neat arrangement of petals and its shining whiteness – soon to be followed by *P. lilacina plena*. Many more were acquired, including old favourites like P. 'William Chalmers' and P. 'Blackbutts Supreme' now no longer to be found. In fifteen years I had a fine collection, not only of *Primula vernales* and its cultivars, but of many other species of primula, including a fine bed of Petiolarids. There are few happier sights than a great drift of *P. Whitei*, ice blue in the thin March sunshine – and even *P. aureata* bloomed happily under the *Cercidiphyllum*.

By this time I had become fascinated by the idea of cross pollination and had several of my own plants, – what fun those first raisings were. In those days they were all 'my babies' and it was difficult to discard a single one.

And then came 1976, with its hot, dry summer. As the fields and hedgerows faded and browned so did my primroses, despite all my care. I set up plastic bottle reservoirs pierced with tiny holes to drip gently beside the plants, and carried endless bowls and buckets out to them. Bathwater was syphoned via the bathroom window into a tank below, and every drop used for cleaning vegetables was saved and used for watering. But as one scorching day followed another, and the burning moor filled the air with the smell of smouldering peat, I watched my plants die and only a few primroses survived. No one was geared up to this kind of extreme heat, and we were totally unprepared. This experience taught me to become much better organised to deal with all kinds of weather though for a brief time I rather wished I had put all my energies into ancient Armenian carols or learning to knit – anything other than primroses. That is what gardening is all about – learning to accept the disappointments as well as the joys. Anyway I was addicted to these plants and over the years had accumulated much research material. So another collection was started, this time with more organisation to combat extremes of weather.

The garden comprises several different areas; in one of these, called 'the plot' (a working area with plunge beds and propagation frames), we set up shade beds, and built wooden frames surrounding two beds upon which green netting is spread in summer. Here, after flowering, I was able to line out the primroses in well prepared soil, with the water tank nearby. Later, as the collection grew, the frames were replaced with a couple of small tunnels. These now house all the 'reserve' primrose plants so that, with many plants growing and flowering in the garden to delight us (and our garden visitors), there are always twice as many in the shelter of the tunnels. Of course, the tunnels are also ideal for young and newly divided plants, and in the hot dry summer of 1989 they housed nearly all the collection.

The next step towards healthy primroses and peace of mind for the gardener came, fortuitously, early in this hot summer of 1989, when I discovered a most efficient automatic watering system that required no electricity and no wastage of water. This is the 'Trinkle' system, which simply requires a small raised tank topped up daily with clean detergent-free water. The flow can be increased or decreased by valves, and in 1989 it kept everything green and healthy.

Some double primroses take unkindly to our very cold, dark, damp winters, so we replace the shade netting with polythene in the winter months, ensuring that it is well supplied with 'windows' for adequate ventilation. This gives us healthy plants to set out in the spring.

One of the great joys of gardening is the friendships it brings; there have been many over the years, both at home and abroad, particularly my 'primrose friends' with whom I have corresponded, swopped plants and spent many happy hours mulling over the pros and cons of various plants, and their treatment. Some have been most generous in passing on old letters, catalogues and notes for my histories of various primroses and those who raised them. It is rather like a jigsaw puzzle – some small piece proving tiresomely elusive, until by happy chance, a snippet of information brings a clue; for instance, once I was showing my illustrations to an artist friend who remembered that 'Lady Greer' was a friend of her mother's and lived in County Kildare – immediately that distant Irish lady after whom the plant was named became a real person.

Among my primrose friends are Mrs Pam Gossage and Mr John Martin who, between them, hold the National Collection of *Primula vernales* and its cultivars in the South of England. It was suggested that, as we all share plants and information very readily and as my collection was comprehensive and already in existence, it might become a duplicate National Collection in the North. Thus, in 1985 my primroses were duly designated the National Collection of *Primula vernales* and its cvs in the North.

The National Council for the Conservation of Plants and Gardens was formed after a two-day conference in October 1978 to consider the problem of saving many of our excellent old cultivars that seemed to be fast disappearing. One result was that a few years later it was decided to set up National Collections, carefully maintained by people who knew what they were doing. Fortunately, the NCCPG has become one of horticulture's success stories, helped by the constant fund raising efforts of a steadily increasing membership. Already, many plants which had almost disappeared can be taken off the endangered list.

So, what difference did becoming a National Collection make to me? I had kept records of my primroses for a number of years, had always tried to keep three of each cultivar and had been used to visitors to the garden, so the difference was not so great. However, it has meant more visitors in primrose time, greatly increased correspondence and many more 'primrose friends'. There is the annual report to write and herbarium specimens to prepare and it is useful to know that the support of the NCCPG is available when needed.

Correct identification is extremely important and this is fascinating detective work that never ends. As a botanical painter I am well used to the close study of plants; endless close observation is the key to discovering their secrets. When comparing two plants the flowers may look much the same, but the calyces or perhaps the backs of the petals may be quite different. Then, of course, there are the other factors to take into consideration – habit, leaf shapes and colours, stems, roots, behaviour, and the plant's provenance and history. Having obtained the complete picture, with what do we compare it? How do we know for certain what the old plants looked like? Past experts may have left written descriptions in books, catalogues and letters, but hardly any quoted the Royal Horticultural Society's colour charts, and one man's 'deep rose' is another man's 'purple'. Sometimes the descriptions given by two people are in complete conflict. The few existing old photographs show little, except whether the flower is single or double, pin-eyed or thrum. However, it is possible to put an accurate name to most things by taking everything into consideration and listing all that has ever been written about a plant by those who knew it well.

This book came about because of my awareness of the lack of accurate primrose pictures for identification. It includes only those primroses which could be correctly identified without any doubt. All gardeners know that there might be slight variations in plants and flowers due to soil conditions, feeding, climate etc, but it is useful to know that these illustrations are a faithful record of plants as they grow in my garden (or occasionally in somebody else's garden) and already several people have found them a useful means of identification.

CHAPTER 2

THE DELIGHT AND CHALLENGE OF BOTANICAL PAINTING

There can be few hobbies more compatible with botanical painting than gardening. Of course, a thorough knowledge of botany is as essential for the botanical artist as a knowledge of anatomy is to the portrait painter, but it is gardening – the daily working among plants, getting to know their ways in all weathers and all seasons – which gives that most helpful, in-depth, intimate knowledge of plants and their life cycle.

The benefits work the other way, too; the painting greatly enhances the gardening. Many hidden beauties among flowers, leaves and stems escape most gardeners, observant as they are of the plants with which they work. They are not always aware of, for instance, the rings of colour deep inside the pearly blue bell of *Codonopsis clematidea*, or the stamens of *Nicotiana langsdorfii* which are an intense peacock blue for a brief day or so before they change colour to gold and brown. How many people seek the beauty of the backs of leaves, or study in detail the infinite variety of seed heads? Yet it is these things, which fill every day's gardening with new discoveries and pleasure for the botanical artist.

More and more people are interested in drawing and painting plants, and yet many keen amateurs feel that they will never achieve recognition without formal art school training. Again, many people in middle age or even retirement have a great desire to paint the plants from either their own garden or the surrounding countryside, but feel dis-couraged by a feeling that they will 'never get anywhere'. Perhaps this account of my own experience will be of help.

My introduction to drawing and painting plants came at a very early age, when an excellent art teacher inculcated discipline and thorough observation right from the beginning. No doubt geometric figures and still life studies played their part in our basic artistic education, but the highlight of my week was Wednesday afternoons when we were allowed to pick a piece of plant material to draw and paint, – a never-ending source of pleasure and variety. When I was nine or ten a couple of my drawings were accepted by the children's academy and hung in London. After this my artistic endeavours were encouraged, but World War II prevented me from continuing studies at art school.

For some years after the war, while bringing up a young family, I dabbled in oil painting; landscapes, still life, abstracts. They gave a lot of pleasure but it was not serious work, and I knew that my detailed technique was too 'tight' for oil painting. This, together with the old 'pull' of working with plants led me to begin a book of all the flowers in our garden, month by month. It was started as a sort of sketch book, but within weeks I was working in more and more detail and was getting tremendous enjoyment from it all. Painting a wide variety of flowers each month as they opened imposed a great discipline – the techniques required for dealing with widely differing shapes, textures and colour had to be mastered, and every page became a challenge. After this I began to show locally and the commissions started coming in. An early commission was to illustrate the little book *Foliage and Form* by Philippa Rakusen which was published in 1974 by the Northern Horticultural Society. This was a great pleasure as foliage is often a greater challenge than flowers, and even stems and bark provide one with endless variety.

As commissions and experience increased, thoughts turned to showing at the Royal Horticultural Society's winter shows in Vincent Square, London. It is said that the RHS shows are to botanical painting what Wimbledon is to tennis, attracting artists from all across the world; certainly showing there is a most worthwhile and valuable experience for any botanical painter.

My first showing in 1977 consisted of six little paintings borrowed from their owners, which I entered just to get the feel of the place and to learn the ropes. To my surprise I was awarded a Grenfell Medal, one of the Grenfell awards for 'botanical pictures, photographs or objects of a similar nature'. The following year I was awarded the Grenfell silver medal for flowers of the various seasons.

This experience gave a better appreciation of exactly what was required to stage a really good exhibition, and for the next show I decided upon a set of conifer paintings, each one a branch or branches, with cones. Interesting and unusual specimens were obtained with help from various botanical gardens etc. Then many months were spent drawing-in and painting the exacting cones, which require almost mathematical calculations to reproduce, and thousands of needles of every size and colour, each with its own minute shadow. At last, in February 1980, we hung the eighteen pictures amid the usual pleasant atmosphere of friendly faces, lovely flowers and heavenly smells, and to my delight they were awarded the RHS gold medal. The pleasure of this occasion was matched some months later, when one of my conifer paintings was given the rare honour of appearing on the front cover of *The Garden*, the journal of the RHS. Many more commissions followed, including work for the

RHS publication *The Plantsman* and various pieces for botanical gardens and collectors. One of the most unusual of these was a beautifully intricate cone of *Keteleeria davidiana* brought back from the 1981 expedition to China led by R. J. Mitchell, with Roy Lancaster. So, botanical illustration is not just painting pretty flowers all the time. It affords a great variety of forms and textures and subtle colouring. The artist is constantly faced with something new and very often exciting to paint.

Apart from exhibiting with the Royal Horticultural Society I have shown at various galleries, and regularly show with the Society of Botanical Artists, the Royal Society of Miniature Painters and the Society of Miniaturists. There is a saying among artists that, when setting out as a professional, it is better to show than to sell, and certainly one learns a lot from seeing one's work alongside that of others, and from mixing with other artists and exchanging ideas. The special 'feel' of a preview is heady stuff for the beginner, a great encouragement to progress further. As an artist becomes established and the commissions book is more constantly full, showing at exhibitions becomes less important, but nevertheless it is good to take part and to see the old red spots appear beside one's work.

If you are thinking of showing at the RHS winter shows, it is important to write for a schedule in very good time, to see exactly what is required and how to apply for space, which is always in great demand. Those with previous awards have priority, but some space is always reserved for first-time exhibitors. Even if you have no intention of working professionally in the future, showing in this way can be stimulating and encouraging, and a good opportunity to learn from more experienced artists, each with a different approach to their subject.

Producing really excellent work requires great concentration. The artist needs peace, quiet and freedom from distraction. Even if you are able to 'switch off' and find stillness when needed, interruptions, discomfort or faulty materials are extremely irritating and disrupting.

Botanical Painting

Not everybody has access to the ideal studio, facing North and lit by windows throwing the light exactly as required, but good light is absolutely essential. In botanical work, because it is so important to get colours exactly right, always paint in daylight; artificial light can be reserved for drawing-in. You should be comfortable at your work, with desk or table at the right height and body well balanced. There is a lot to be said for the Japanese instruction for painting which begins, 'first rest your left arm on the table'. (This was brought home to me recently when my left arm was in plaster and I found that the 'ease' had gone from working.) For drawing, use HB pencils sharpened to a very fine point to produce only the lightest of lines. I keep several dozen and change them frequently so that outlines are sharp and clear; this is especially essential for fine points like stamens and nectaries. Clear and accurate drawing-in is worthwhile, as flowers can change position during the course of the work without the artist noticing, and you can compensate without being aware of doing so.

The type of paper used is a matter of personal choice. Many botanical artists use a hot-pressed flat paper because of the fineness of the work, but I generally favour a slightly textured paper which gives more life to the picture. Whatever materials you use, always aim for the very best quality.

Paint should be good artists' quality, and a wide variety of colours is essential (I often have four ceramic palettes on the go at the same time). For instance, one plant may need a great many shades of green to reproduce all the nuances and shadows, and this may require several greens mixed with other colours.

Excellent brushes are of the greatest importance – I always use Kolynsky sable, frequently renewed. For most botanical work, 000 and 00 brushes are best, though a size 1 or 2 is useful for large leaves in bigger pictures. Painting on vellum is enjoyable, especially for small pictures and miniature work. The finest calf is appropriate for most subjects but it is interesting to experiment: a rather veiny sheep vellum can be used to good effect and bold chunky subjects such as cones look effective on very grainy natural goatskin.

Ivory is no longer an acceptable material, but there is a good substitute called Ivorine which has the right translucent quality.

The very essence of botanical painting (as against the looser concept of flower painting in general) is that the work should be botanically correct in every detail. For that reason the most useful piece of equipment is a ×8 magnifying glass, attached to a swivelled arm fixed to the work table or held in the left hand. Of course, many artists will feel that their sight is so good that a magnifier is unnecessary but it is really essential for examining, drawing and painting such things as stamens and fine hairs. How often one sees a well executed flower painting ruined by stamens that are indicated by coarse blobs about the centre, or hairs on a stem all going in the wrong direction. These small details make such a great difference to a piece of work. One should beware, though, of drawing in larger areas of a plant under the glass, for it is possible to end up with the whole thing out of proportion or miniaturised.

Apart from rare occasions when I have had to work from earlier studies, I always paint from life. The result is more true and lively and avoids some nasty pitfalls. Some people paint from photographs but photography can never capture quite the same quality as botanical painting and certainly even the best cannot always match the same true colour and detail, which must be why botanical painting still flourishes. There are those who use their own studies for later selection of material, but there are pitfalls with this method; a fellow artist once told me that he had put the wrong type of acorns on a spray of oak leaves, and there is a fine book on a well known garden which has an illustration showing pin-eyed and thrum-eyed flowers both on one primrose plant – this of course never occurs in nature.

Working from life does have its problems. The fine clump of hellebores in an ideal state for painting tomorrow will be found, when tomorrow comes, to be frozen solid under inches of snow. You will watch carefully for the opening of some ephemeral flower that must be painted with all speed and then be faced with a leaden sky like the

Day of Judgement and absolutely no light to work by. Buds can open at the most inconvenient times, but they can be held back for a few hours, by placing them in water in the refrigerator, which should be kept at a fairly high temperature (ie not too cold). Most of these problems can be solved with a little ingenuity, and it pays never to drop standards or to take shortcuts. The finished work will prove that it was worthwhile.

Some illustrations require only the flowers and leaves, which can be picked and kept in water while being painted. Others need to include the roots, so the plant must be dug up together with its surrounding soil and kept in the growing state for some time. These I put in a shallow dish with wet tissue over the roots and soil. The plant is sprayed from time to time and the roots moistened. The natural demands of your specimens must be considered. They must 'go to bed' at the right time and must not be left under bright lights until late at night. A shade lover should not be left in brilliant sunlight, and no plant should be left in a warm room for any length of time. Work on the flowers and buds first and finish them before painting the leaves, which will deteriorate less quickly. If you want to add an 'extra', such as the forming seedhead of a flower that has finished, plan its position etc, but concentrate on painting the parts that are ready.

When ready to paint the roots, shake off the soil carefully (helped by the judicious use of a skewer), wash them well, and lay the whole plant in a flat dish with a pad of wet tissue under the roots. Work rapidly until they are finished!

When the work is finished, if the weather is warm and favourable, the plant can be replanted outside. This is best done in the evening so that it is in no way distressed by strong sunlight soon after planting. It should be watered, and, if there is a likelihood of strong winds or hot sun, sheltered with a little shade netting. In winter it may be necessary to pot-up the plant and put it temporarily into a cold frame (or other sheltered site) if the weather is very cold or the ground hard.

Hellebores are one of the most popular groups of winter flowering plants, which I am often asked to paint. They are planted outside again as soon as conditions are favourable. It is most interesting, from a gardener's point of view, that none of the hellebores has ever resented being treated in this way. All have settled in happily and continued to flower, which is particularly surprising with hellebores. I sometimes think that, coming up so often, they regard it as part of life, like having a holiday!

Occasionally the commissioned picture is for a painting of some rare or special plant raised or collected by the person concerned. On these occasions the material is brought or sent at rather short notice and then it is a case of dropping everything else and giving it full attention at once. Sometimes the poor thing has flagged on its journey, but nearly always a long drink in deep water in cool surroundings will soon revive it. When requests are made for plants which are not in the garden other gardeners may provide a specimen or, horticultural and botanic gardens may be persuaded to help.

Perhaps the most important word in the botanical painter's dictionary is observation. Good work can be spoilt by lack of attention to detail, because the artist simply has not noticed some of the finer points. It is easy to see a plant, or a species, in a preconceived way, as a whole, without seeing the variations within it. For instance, we may think of *Primula vulgaris* leaves as being very deeply veined and rugose, but some are much less indented, with leaves that are almost smooth. Plants vary and even all the leaves on the same plant will show a difference in shapes and surfaces. Primrose leaves tend to get smoother as they get older, the younger leaves being more deeply indented, but the opposite can apply – sometimes old leaves are very heavily puckered and rugose and, occasionally, young leaves are fairly smooth. So, it pays to take nothing for granted.

If painting, for instance, the primrose 'Bon Accord Purple' I would always paint the leaves from that particular plant. The leaves of 'Bon Accord Gem' would not do equally well even though they look almost identical – each flower should have its own foliage. Faced with painting hundreds of leaves for the illustrations in this book, it might have been tempting to make do with the ones that were to hand at the time, especially as I had to finish off the foliage on several plants one after the other; but it was definitely worthwhile to discard each plant's leaves as its painting was finished and start the next illustration with a fresh approach. This sort of thing makes for satisfactory work.

Of course, not only the flowers and leaves must be accurately depicted; the aim is to capture the nature of the whole plant – its personality and behaviour. Study the subject carefully. Are the stems rather lax and floppy, or do the flowers stand up above the leaves? Perhaps they tend to nestle down so they are almost hidden. We may think that all hellebores hang their heads in chaste fashion, but some are bold and upward looking. This kind of observation is vital, for a well executed painting can come over as flat and lifeless if the essential character of the plant is lost. And it does happen – I have even seen gorse depicted with gently undulating stems and side branches!

Amateur artists often ask whether or not to put blemished leaves, flowers or other parts of a plant, into a picture. This varies with the type of plant and the type of picture. When working upon a large and decorative picture of, say, fine large peonies or oriental poppies, it is better to keep the whole thing free of blemishes. In the garden, the general effect of a tree peony or a fine clump of oriental poppies at flowering time is of the full health and beauty of summertime, and that is the impression that should be conveyed, because somehow it is the very essence of those flowers.

Do not paint a diseased or chlorotic plant – not only would it be unpleasing but it would not be typical of the plant. For this reason, ignore damage by slugs or caterpillars. However, where blemished or distorted leaves are very much a part of a plant, put one or two in. Primroses hold their leaves over a long period and if left to themselves will almost always have one or more yellowing or patchy leaves at the base of the plant – even in spring and early summer. It is acceptable to show these, within reason, as they are part of the nature of the plant. Other plants also

have certain manifestations, the leaves of *Geranium palmatum* bend downwards with age until they lie along the soil; some might find this unsightly but this is as much a part of the plant's behaviour as the flowers of *Allium siculum* that bend down as the bloom unfolds and turn up again when it has finished flowering. Such things are part of a plant's life cycle, contributing to the infinite variety of nature.

Some people ask how much specimens may be 'arranged' to produce a more artistically pleasing picture. A plant should be 'prettified' only in so far as it does not interfere with the nature of that plant. To remove a large leaf that obscures several flowers is one thing, to thin out most of the foliage on an otherwise leafy specimen produces a false impression – as does elongating the stems of flowers that normally nestle among their leaves to make them seem more striking for the picture. Such actions must be avoided; however for a couple of centuries many botanical painters have left certain parts of a subject drawn in but not coloured. With a very crowded specimen, where there are crossed stems and layers of leaves, this helps to show the essential parts of the plant. Also, it is aesthetically pleasing to vary the treatment of parts of a very fussy plant – indeed I have seen superb pictures by Georg Dionysius Ehret in which the whole of the stems and leaves were drawn in and just a few flowers were painted.

Very often I find leaves are more of a challenge than most flowers. Their often very subtle colouring can range from darkest purple through flame, blue, green and gold to palest parchment. Their textures vary from the firm and glossy, almost waxy, surfaces of camellias (and *Hoya carnosa* with its sharp flashing highlights) to dull leaves, almost like mottled suede, as in the sages. There are felty leaves, spiny or downright hairy leaves, and others that are deeply ridged or heavily indented as with the *vulgaris* primroses. Veins painted as lines upon a finished leaf make me feel that the painter has missed a chance to add life and texture to that leaf. I can think of no leaf which, in nature, has its veins simply as lines upon a flat surface – most veins are to some extent recessed and must therefore produce a shadow alongside, sharing either a shallow or deep indentation. Likewise the leaves with slightly raised veins, like the central ribs of camellias, also throw a shadow along one side, which accentuates the rib.

It is well to remember when painting plants in general, and primroses in particular, that all the leaves on the same plant are not necessarily of the same colour. Certain plants are said to have leaves of a certain colour – *P. alba plena* has a nice fresh green leaf, *P.* 'Our Pat' has very distinctive pinky bronze leaves, while *P.* 'Guinevere' has purple tinged leaves. These are typical of the plant and make it easily identifiable, and yet if you look closely many of the leaves are different colours. Very often there is quite a colour difference between young and old leaves. Also, those which have been overlaid by other leaves can be quite a different colour. This is particularly true in the case of red or purple tinted leaves; the under foliage of *Acer dissectum atropurpureum* may often be found to be quite green, while that on top is a rich red. Two plants of the same variety may also vary quite noticeably, depending upon soil conditions, situation and the general health and well being of the plant.

The leaf margins also vary within the plant. Whether dentate or crenate, primrose leaves have a habit of becoming quite irregular, and very often the 'teeth' disappear altogether. This is particularly noticeable when drawing in the leaves of *P. juliae* – some have teeth like dragons while others appear to have no more than gums, and one leaf alone may vary from smooth to toothed. This illustrates the folly of taking one or two leaves and basing the whole plant portrait upon those, for it will not ring true.

Likewise, roots also vary greatly. Obviously the roots of *vulgaris* type primroses and *juliae* type are very different in structure, but the roots of one type will vary from plant to plant, depending upon moisture, the conditions below the plant, and the stage of growth. After flowering, primroses put out new roots right under the crown at the neck of the plant. So it is always worthwhile obtaining the correct root to draw from.

It would be impossible to enter into all the intricacies of colour mixing here, but one or two pointers may be helpful. A useful practice for someone in the early stages of botanical painting is to collect half a dozen leaves of very different shades of green and mix the colour for each, by trial and error, noting down the components of each mixture for future reference. You can carry this further to cover red, bronze leaves, etc, so that eventually you may handle with confidence any foliage that presents itself. Some glaucous leaf shades in particular take a great deal of 'finding' on the palette; it is worthwhile spending time practising with these so that you are prepared when the opportunity arises to paint, for example, a nice branch of *Eucalyptus* or *Ruta graveolens*.

When colour mixing for reddish and purple leaves, bear in mind that over-mixing can result in a very muddy effect, and a far livelier look may be obtained by not mixing the paints too thoroughly. Where a leaf gives the appearance of being suffused with red or gold, try painting the surface an underlying green and when quite dry giving it a very quick, light wash over with the desired colour.

Remember when painting flowers that all flowers on one plant will not necessarily be the same colour. As flowers age their colours often change; I have even seen pinks change the shape of their lacings as days went by. Often, because of these changes, when painting for identification purposes, I will indicate the age of the flower, eg second day. Likewise, with primroses, late flowers may not be by any means typical. In the autumn quite a variety of doubles become semi-single, and plain named singles become semi-double, fringed or frilled in a most frivolous fashion. For this reason I would never choose to paint them if wishing to convey the true picture and you should always bear these factors in mind when identifying plants.

It is impossible to over-stress the value of experiment, whether with colours or techniques. Try a gum-and-water vehicle to produce a rich velvety texture on things like auriculas and pinks, or diluted inks for tissue-thin, translucent poppy petals. Practise putting a bloom on a grape and hairs on a gooseberry – the enjoyment is endless.

CHAPTER 3

THE PRIMROSES

It would be difficult to imagine a time without primroses. By the Middle Ages they were being praised in literature by poets and playwrights - the name 'prime flower' meaning the fairest and best, as in Edmund Spenser's later lines:

'As fairer nymph yet never saw mine eie
She is the pride and primrose of the rest'.

Both primroses and cowslips were used medicinally from very early times. Leonardo da Vinci said that primrose leaves were very appetising, but not very digestible; boiled, they were good for stones in the bladder. Culpepper in *The Complete Herbal*, advised the use of leaves made into 'as fine a salve to heal wounds as any that I know', whilst Gerard in his *Herball* of 1597 advised the boiled leaves for 'Phrensie', and the roots 'stamped and strained, and the juice sniffed into the nose . . . purgeth the brain and qualifieth the pain of the megrim'.

Whilst not indulging in any of these cures, I have, in my youth, taken both primrose and cowslip wine. There was also a cowslip cream, which was very delicately flavoured. Primrose flowers were candied on occasions; particularly for Mothering Sunday.

The name *Primula veris* appeared in 1101 in *'Regimen Sanitas Salerni'* as one of the plants used for the cure of paralysis, and the name cowslip goes back probably further than AD1000 when it was known as Cu Slyppen and Cu Sloppe. It also enjoyed the old common name of 'Paigle', which endured in country districts well into this century. Gerard wrote of the 'double Paigle the English garden cowslip', and another, which he calls a 'double cowslip' but which is obviously a hose-in-hose form for he says 'Having but one floure within another, which maketh the same once double, whereas the other (the double paigle) is many times double, called by *Pena, Geminata* for the likeness of the floures, which are brought forth as things against nature, or twinnes.'

Primula veris (see page 18) crosses with *Primula vulgaris* (see page 17) naturally in the wild and the resulting *P. variabilis* is quite commonly found in areas where both parents flourish together. This plant, sometimes called the false oxlip, is, as its name suggests, very variable, being a chance cross, and is not to be confused with the true oxlip, *P. elatior* (see page 19). These hybrids were the forebears of the polyanthus, from the Greek *polyanthos* meaning many flowered, and also of the polyanthus type primrose.

It is obvious from the work of many early writers that primroses had 'come into the garden' by the late Middle Ages and also that there were many forms. Tabernaemontanus described a double yellow primrose in 1500. Parkinson, writing his *Paradisi in Sole* in 1629, describing what he calls 'the ordinary double primrose' says 'the leaves are very large and like unto the single kind but somewhat larger because it groweth in gardens'. From this we may deduce that double primroses were quite common in gardens. (It seems to be the Double Sulphur (see page 28) that he was describing.)

As far as we know, the oldest of all the double primroses is *Primula vulgaris alba plena* (see page 20) together with the double yellow. It is the loveliest of all the doubles, with petals arranged rather symmetrically in a rosette, and is of the purest white. Gerard refers to it in his *Herball* as 'Of all the rest the greatest beautie,' and for this reason our old classic, *P. alba plena*, has often been called 'Gerard's double white'. Some people now say that Gerard cannot have been referring to the *P. alba plena* that we know, as the illustration in the *Herball* shows a polyanthus-type umbel with a marked scape protruding above the leaves. It is as well to remember that many of the wood-cuts in our old herbals bore little relation to the plant under consideration; some were made from old blocks re-cut and sometimes reversed, and others were 'lifted' from other books. The *Herbal and Bestiary* produced between 1510 and 1520 contains a wood-cut of a *Primula veris* with long, swirling almost strap-shaped leaves, for instance, and we know that very few of the illustrations in the *Herball* of 1597 were originals produced to accompany the text. Nearly 1,800 were obtained from Tabernaemontanus's Frankfurt publishers and John Gerard was called upon to produce the text to accompany them – and hurriedly at that.

Since we know that these wood-cut blocks were being lent and passed around, it would be worth knowing whether blocks destined for the Plantin Press publication of Clusius's work of 1583 and, again, his *Rariorum Plantarium Historia* of 1601 could have appeared in the *Herball*, as Clusuis writes of *Primula veris vulgaris alba flore pleno*, to gether with a red one, and these were presumably polyanthus-type doubles since he names it *veris vulgaris*. This is of course pure speculation but makes for interesting discussion.

There were also, at this time, a number of what are known as anomalous primroses and polyanthus (see page 24). These are plants with flowers whose calyces deviate from the normal form. In the hose-in-hose the calyx becomes petaloid, so that the effect is of one flower emerging from another in the manner of the dress of a Tudor man who might wear two pairs of hose, one turned down over the other. In the Jack-in-the-Green, the calyx becomes foliaceous and gives the flower the appearance of nestling in a circlet of leaves. Jack-in-the-Greens come with both single and double flowers. There is a very showy single called 'Salamander' (see page 25) of a rich glowing red and, by contrast, 'Tipperary Purple' (see page 26), a gentle little primrose with flowers of pinky lilac – a very sturdy plant which increases well. A modern double form is *P.* 'Dawn Ansell' (see page 27), with huge green 'ruffs'. Jackanapes is a form of Jack-in-the-Green where the leafy calyx is irregularly streaked with the same colour as the petals of the flower, giving a rather showy effect. There are also other variations called Jackanapes-on-Horseback, Galligaskins and Pantaloons; all have some kind of distortion of the calyx, but accounts vary, and it would be difficult to describe positively any one of them.

There has been a considerable range of colour in our garden primroses for a very long time. Clusius's reference to *P. veris vulgaris rubra flore pleno* in 1601 has already been mentioned, and Parkinson, writing in 1640, told of a red primrose, *P. vulgaris rubra* brought over from Turkey, his oft-quoted primrose of 'Turkie-purple'. This was presumably a dark form of *P. vulgaris* subsp. *sibthorpii* (see page 21) which came in shades of pink, red or purple. Dr McWatt, writing in 1923, stated that *P. sibthorpii* is the parent of all our coloured primroses; and though this is not altogether correct, there being so many other factors involved, it has certainly played a very big part in primrose development. *P. sibthorpii*, found in Greece, The Caucasus and Northern Persia, was used by many primrose growers to raise plants of new colours and sound constitution. *P. vulg. subsp. heterochroma*, which is indigenous to Northern Persia and whose flowers are white, purple, blue and yellow, was introduced also into the primrose breeding programme, but not so extensively, and one does not see it today.

It has been suggested that the lovely old double primrose *P. lilacina plena* (see page 22), syn. *P.* 'Quaker's Bonnet' – which dates back to the eighteenth century – is the double form of *P. sibthorpii*. This is what I had always believed until I saw a very large, single lilac primrose of the exact colour and with a distinctive white rim to its yellow eye in the famous Margery Fish garden at East Lambrook Manor. I was told that it was considered to be the single form of *P. lilacina plena*. This identification seems much more likely as, if the petals of the double are pulled apart, it shows that the yellow eye at the base of the petal has a clear white edge, which is absent in *P. sibthorpii*. Miss Eda Hume wrote to Mrs McMurtrie in 1955 of a lilac primrose 'which was always called "Belvedere"' and Amos Perry, listing the primroses in their catalogue for 1895 in a letter to William Chalmers, mention 'Belvedere Lilac'. Roy Genders describes 'Belvedere' as 'of immense size' and interestingly, Mrs McMurtrie on going through old personal papers noted that 'Belvedere' was the single form of *P. lilacina plena*.

In the wild, too, the occurrence of coloured forms of *P. vulgaris* seems to have been far from uncommon. I remember in the twenties often picking posies of primroses in shades of pink, whilst white was very common. In *Field Flowers* (1870) Shirley Hibberd wrote of seeing

> in Devonshire and Somersetshire, great circular clumps of wild primroses, covering sometimes as much as a hundred square yards each, and comprising flowers of fifty different hues. Sometimes in these clumps there is not one yellow or yellowish white flower . . . but we shall find palest lilac, delicate rose, rich purple and sometimes a rare and curious tint of blue.

He also mentioned a primrose in which colours became mixed to produce 'an indescribable dirty brown colour – a primrose almost obnoxious to the sight'. I do not know how widely travelled Shirley Hibberd was, but it is interesting to note that he felt that this range of colours was found more frequently in the West Country and that 'yellow and white flowers prevailed in the Midlands and East of England'.

Double flowers, too, appear in the wild. The modern double *P.* 'Sue Jervis' (see page 30) was found in the wild and marketed by Bressingham about 1980; a vigorous grower, it has delicate salmon-pink flowers which I find a rather subtle colour but some consider plain dingy.

About 1930 an eight-year-old child named Elizabeth Dickey found a charming double yellow primrose growing near her home about two miles from Ballymoney in Northern Ireland. She took it home to her mother who kept it thriving in her garden for some thirty years when it came to the notice of Dr Molly Sanderson, the well known Irish

gardener. She named it 'Elizabeth Dickey', and sent a plant to that renowned primrose grower David Chalmers at West Blackbutts Nursery, near Stonehaven, since when it has flourished and been distributed. Dr Sanderson also sent over another double yellow which was found in the Boyne Valley. She told me that there was a 'bank with a great population of primroses, nearly all double' – imagine finding such a treasure. She named this second primrose 'Boyne Valley'. Although similar to 'Elizabeth Dickey' there are differences; the leaf seems to be rather smoother for one thing, and 'Boyne Valley' is not such a strong grower although a good flowerer.

Another primrose known since the days of Gerard is the green primrose *P. viridis*, both single and double. These vary; usually the petals are welted making them rather leafy in form, but there is another form with more of a pure flower, which has typical petals of delicate texture and which are nicked at the rim. The plant in the illustration (see page 23) was growing at East Lambrook Manor and had both single and semi-double flowers upon it.

The development of the polyanthus is possibly even less clear than that of the primrose. The Rev Samuel Gilbert writing in *The Florist's Vade Mecum* (1683) told of his polyanthus which were in shades of red. One assumes that these were derived from red *P. variabilis*, or from red primroses. True polyanthus have been selectively bred for more than 300 years, but some of the modern varieties with their brilliant colours and enormous flowers bear little relation to their early ancestors.

Of all the varieties of polyanthus, perhaps the most outstanding for their charm and classic beauty are the gold-laced (see page 31). Again it is impossible to say just when these were developed. Dr McWatt wrote that Abercrombie in 1778 mentioned, if not gold-laced varieties, something approaching them. Certainly, by the middle of the nineteenth century the raising and showing of them had fired florists with such enthusiasm that rules were drawn up as to exactly how the perfect flowers should appear. In the North of England, the competition among florists was

Thrum eye

Pin eye

PLATE 1

Primula vulgaris

17

PLATE 2

P. veris

18

PLATE 5

P. vulgaris subsp. *sibthorpii*

21

PLATE 6

1. 'Belvedere' 2. P. lilacina plena

22

PLATE 7

P. viridis

23

1. *Jackanapes*

2. *Hose-in-Hose*

3. *Jack-in-the-Green*

PLATE 8

Anomalous Primroses

24

PLATE 9

'Salamander'

25

PLATE 10
'Tipperary Purple'
26

PLATE 11

'Dawn Ansell'

27

PLATE 12

'Double Sulphur'

28

PLATE 15

'Gold-laced Polyanthus'

31

PLATE 16

'Barrowby Gem'

32

PLATE 17

'Marie Crousse'

33

PLATE 18

'Prince Silverwings'

34

PLATE 19

'Chevithorne Pink'

35

PLATE 20

'Bon Accord Cerise'

36

PLATE 21

'Bon Accord Lavender'

37

PLATE 22

'Bon Accord Purple'

38

PLATE 23
'Fife Yellow'
39

PLATE 24
'Paddy'

40

PLATE 27

'Guinevere'

43

PLATE 28
'Enchantress'

44

PLATE 29

'Lopen Red'

45

PLATE 30

'Lambrook Pink'

46

1. *Hose-in-Hose*

2. *Jack-in-the-Green*

PLATE 33
'*Wanda*'

49

PLATE 34
'Perle von Bottrop'

50

PLATE 39

'*White Wanda*'

55

PLATE 40

'Queen of the Whites'

56

PLATE 41

'Our Pat'

57

PLATE 42

'Kinlough Beauty'

58

PLATE 43

'Lady Greer'

59

PLATE 44
'Dorothy'

60

PLATE 45

'McWatt's Claret'

61

PLATE 46

'Iris Mainwaring'

62

PLATE 49

'Blue Riband'

65

PLATE 50
'David Green'

66

PLATE 51

'Buckland Wine'

67

PLATE 52

'Dr Molly'

68

PLATE 53

'Lingwood Beauty'

69

PLATE 54
'Tomato Red'

70

PLATE 55

'Ingram's Blue'

71

1

2

3

PLATE 56

1. 'Paris 90' 2. 'Striped Victorian' 3. 'Chartreuse'

PLATE 57

'Miss Indigo'

73

PLATE 58
'Lillian Harvey'

74

PLATE 59

'Eugenie'

75

PLATE 60

'Corporal Baxter'

76

PLATE 61

'Ken Dearman'

77

PLATE 62

'Sunshine Susie'

78

PLATE 63

'Rhapsody'

79

PLATE 64

'Ladybird'

80

acute. The body colour can vary from light-brownish-red through varying shades of crimson to almost black, and the eyes and lacings from a deep gold to the palest silver.

There are many polyanthus-type primroses in which the flowers are borne in an umbel, arising from a scape, which may vary in length or be absent. These were known as bunch primroses. The lovely single yellow 'Barrowby Gem' (see page 32) which came from Barrowby Hall in East Yorkshire is a real polyanthus-type primrose. It has a greenish eye and a delicious fragrance – the first to come into flower, it embodies all that one could wish for in a herald of spring. This is a fairly old variety. Mr Roger, from whom I acquired my plants some years ago, told me that they have certainly been growing in his garden since the 1930s.

Whilst some primroses in the latter half of the last century were named after people, places, etc, they were more generally known by their colours, 'Double Cream', 'French Grey', 'Dingy' and so forth, and it is only comparatively recently that all primroses have received proper names. One of the oldest of the named polyanthus-primroses in cultivation today is *P.* 'Marie Crousse' (see page 33) introduced from France, which won a Royal Horticultural Society award of merit in 1882. There seems to have been two varieties of 'Marie Crousse', one deep red and one of a lilac purple. Like so many colour variations, these could be due to soil conditions, but in *The Garden* of 1902 Helen Champernowne wrote of a paler one flowering earlier and having a different habit from the crimson one, which was very late to bloom – so probably there were two distinct varieties at that time. The flowers are splashed and edged with white, fully double and profuse, upon short polyanthus stems, often with true primroses arising from the base on single pedicels on the same plant. 'Marie Crousse' is a vigorous grower and may produce great large-leaved crowns in a comparatively short time. It has also been called 'Crousse Plena'.

Another very old variety is 'Prince Silverwings' (see page 34) raised by T. Smith of Newry in 1897. A polyanthus-primrose described by the Rev P. H. Mules in *The Garden* in 1898, it tends to bear single blooms for a time after dividing until established, and often one may find flowers that vary from fully double to almost single on one plant. This is a very rare primrose; I searched for it for many years before finding it at East Lambrook Manor. After having seen some so-called 'Prince Silverwings' – which clearly were not – it was a pleasure to find the true plant. Not only does it fit all descriptions, in colour and in having the orange spot at the base of the petal, but its provenance clinched the matter. It had come from Ledbury, the garden of the late Percy Picton who certainly had it there. This primrose sometimes produces pollen in its more single flowers and is useful for crossing with other primroses.

'Chevithorne Pink' (see page 35) is another charming old 'bunch primrose'. There has been some confusion as to where it was raised partly because, for some obscure reason, it was given almost the same name as a primrose raised thirty years before in the nineteen twenties. Dr C. E. Nelson of Glasnevin Botanical Gardens reported that 'Chevithorne Pink' was raised by Mrs Elison Spence of Co Tyrone about 1950 and was named by Mrs Emmerson, who ran a well known nursery at Limavady. However there is no doubt that 'Chevithorne Purple' was raised at Chevithorne Barton near Tiverton in Devon. Mrs Emmerson wrote to Mrs McMurtrie in 1952, 'Mrs Amory did not raise it but found it in the garden, it is now no longer there. Possibly quite an old primrose?' H. G. Moore, in the National Auricula & Primula Society's Diamond Jubilee Year Report (1936), mentioned 'Chevithorne' in a list of polyanthus-primroses. Whilst 'Chevithorne Pink' still flourishes, and is one of the prettiest of our doubles, 'Chevithorne Purple' seems to have disappeared long ago.

Perhaps some of the best known polyanthus-primroses of all were the 'Bon Accord' primroses, raised about 1900 by William Cocker of Aberdeen, a renowned rose-grower. Early in this century there were several splendid primrose growers living in the north east of Scotland – William Chalmers at West Blackbutts, Murray Thompson, of Kingennie, Angus who raised the 'Downshill' group, the

Cocker brothers and those reverend gentlemen, John McMurtrie and William Murdoch – a wealth of good primroses have come from manse and rectory over the years. The Rev Murdoch, writing in the annual report of the National Auricula & Primula Society Southern Section in 1935, did not think much of the name chosen for the 'Bon Accords'. He said of William Cocker

'he sent them out with the terrible name "Bon Accord Hybrid Primrose", Bon Accord being the motto of the city of Aberdeen, plantsmen called them Cocker's Bon Accord Hybrids and since the name was long it became split up and collectors in some parts say they have Cockers and so many Bon Accords, not knowing that they are one and the same thing.'

There were about fourteen different Bon Accords originally. Some of them are very similar, for instance, 'Bon Accord Gem' and 'Bon Accord Cerise' (see page 36) of which Mr Murdoch wrote, 'it was a pity Cocker made these two for they are practically identical'. However most of them have disappeared, which is a pity. I especially like the sound of 'Bon Accord Purity', which was an excellent white tinged with green. Apart from 'Bon Accord Gem' and 'Bon Accord Cerise', we still have 'Bon Accord Purple' (see page 38) and 'Bon Accord Lavender' (see page 37). T. A. Townsend, nurseryman at Forest Town, Mansfield, was one of the few people to use the Royal Horticultural Society's colour charts when describing some of his primroses, and he gave the colour of 'Bon Accord Lavender' as Dauphin's violet (039/3). It is most interesting to note that after all these years and many changes of soil the flowers on my plants of this are exactly that colour.

From that north eastern area of Scotland David Chalmers, who carried on in the fine tradition of his father, found a rich yellow double which he named 'Fife Yellow' (see page 39). This primrose varies in colour from quite a deep ochre shade earlier in the season to a lighter colour shaded to almost orange at the base, as in the illustration. It is perhaps worth mentioning here that in 1935 Mr Smith of Newry sent the Rev McMurtrie what he called a double 'orange-yellow'

polyanthus-type primrose which he later named 'Maize Yellow', so that would have been around in north eastern Scotland. Without making any claims, it is interesting to speculate about 'Fife Yellow' which Mrs McMurtrie, upon seeing my illustration, said was very like 'Maize Yellow'.

One more of the older double polyanthus-primroses is 'Paddy' (see page 40), also known as *P. rubra plena*, *P. sanguinea plena*, 'Crimson Paddy' and 'Irish Paddy', bred in 1897 by that raiser of so many fine primroses T. Smith of Newry who called it 'Paddy' (the 'Irish' seems to have been added to it later to denote its origin). It is a good red, frosted white at the petal edges. Sometimes the later flowers will be less double and will produce pollen.

One of the most momentous days in the history of the primrose must have been the day in April 1900 when Julia Ludovikovna Mlokossjewicz came across a little purple-flowered primula near Lagodechy some eighty miles east-north-east of Tiflis in the province of Georgia in the Caucasus. This she named *Primula juliae* (see page 41) and it became what Margery Fish called 'The mother of them all', being used in the raising of most of the coloured primroses we have today. This little plant went into cultivation quite soon. It was forwarded by Kusnetzow to the botanical gardens at Oxford and Kew in 1911-12, and appeared in the *Botanical Magazine*. Balfour received living plants at Edinburgh Botanics in 1912.

We are, perhaps, too apt to pigeon-hole events into dates without realising that individuals may make something of a nonsense of this. *P. juliae* is said to have come to this country about 1911 but Nancy Lindsey, a most knowledgeable gardener who ran her nursery at Manor Cottage, Sutton Courteney, wrote about

'P. Juliana "Craven Bells" – given by Farrer to my mother when I was a child as "my favourite cowslip". Mr Robinson of Oxford Botanical Gardens was sure it was a *juliae* hybrid, which seemed impossible if *P. juliae* had only been introduced into England around 1912 but Mr Robinson found that Farrer had apparently possessed *P. juliae* already in 1902. "Craven Bells" is a pet – mat-forming Juliana with little lettuce-green leaves and bunches of little ivory-lemon "cowslips" on three-inch stems.'

This is so interesting, not only because it shows that *P. juliae* was, as one might suppose, passed around among the cognoscenti very early in this century, but that the charming little plant, not often seen, which we know as 'Craven Gem' (see page 42) is almost certainly Farrer's 'Craven Bells'.

Another particularly noteworthy event in the development of the coloured varieties was the arrival of the so-called Garryard primroses. These were raised by J. Whiteside-Dane in Garryard Co Kildare – in 1895, according to Hecker, but between 1912 and 1919 according to Dr Nelson. The first of these was 'Appleblossom', of polyanthus type, with flowers of pink and white with red stems and outstanding leaves of a distinctive reddish bronze. This was apparently followed by 'Garryard', described as a polyanthus type with mauve-pink flowers with a yellow eye, with stems and foliage the same as 'Appleblossom'. Dr Nelson believes this to be the same plant as the one we call 'Guinevere' (see page 43), with *P. sibthorpii* a probable parent. It is a fine vigorous grower and, with its purple-stained leaves, is an asset at any time of the year; it looks rather good underplanting 'Queen of the Night' tulips.

Another primrose of the Garryard type is 'Enchantress' (see page 44), a fairly large flower, which gives the impression of being creamy overlaid and grained with a rich pink, and looks particularly well set against the red-stained leaves. There were several so-called Garryard primroses, but the only ones I have had were 'The Grail', a charming old red-brick colour, and 'Sir Galahad', which has rather ruffled petals and is supposed to be white 'Because his heart was pure' but mine is tinged with pink. Hill View nurseries in a 1960s catalogue offered a 'Sir Galahad' of palest pink 'probably not the true plant as the original is reputed to be white'. Roy Genders in his 'Handbook of Primroses', which offers plants from his nursery at Hillway, Scarborough, lists his 'Sir Galahad' as having 'blush-white flowers with attractively frilled petals', so there seems to have been a

pinkish primrose of that name about for a very long time.

Other plants with the splendid bronzy-red leaves akin to 'Guinevere' are sometimes given the prefix 'Garryard' erroneously. One such is the cheerful 'Lopen Red' (see page 45), which was presumably one of Margery Fish's primroses. Other primroses to come out of Mrs Fish's garden were 'Lambrook Lilac', 'Lambrook Yellow', 'Lambrook Pink', (see page 46) and 'Lambrook Peach' (see page 47), charming primroses all of them, but 'Lambrook Peach' is particularly striking with its rich-red calyces and stems and pale-peach flowers.

Once *P. juliae* had come into circulation, primrose growers soon saw the value of it as a parent and the flood of new Juliana hybrids (as they were called) started. Some have come from Holland, and in Germany Herr G. Arends, crossing *P. juliae* with various coloured forms of *P. vulgaris*, produced hybrids which he called *P. x helenae*; these were marketed some time after 1913. One of these was 'Betty Green' (see page 48), another was, according to some sources, *P.* 'Wanda' (see page 49), which I had always believed to be one of the first of the *P. juliae* hybrids. However, Mrs Emmerson of Limavady put in her 1967 list that 'Wanda' evolved at Wolverhampton about 1920. The ubiquitous *P.* 'Wanda' is probably the best known of all the *P. juliae* hybrids and for that reason despised by some, but in the right place it is a cheerful sight on a spring morning and it is so accommodating that it will grow and flower almost anywhere. There are hose-in-hose and Jack-in-the-Green forms and also two newer forms 'Wanda Improved' and 'Wanda's Rival', the latter introduced by Champernowne. These have slightly larger flowers and richer colours.

Another German who was hybridising *P. juliae* was F. Zeeman in Pruhonitz; he named his plants *P. pruhonitziana*, since when some growers have called all *P. juliae* hybrids by this name, but with many the parentage is so complicated it is impossible to say just what they are. Among other *juliae* hybrids to come from Holland and Germany is 'Perle von Bottrop' (see page 50), a Dutch hybrid, which is very showy with rich purple flowers. Another good Dutch variety,

'Groenekins Glory' (see page 51), a pinky lilac with a green eye, is a neat plant which seems to flourish anywhere; and from Germany 'Frühlingzauber' is an early flowering primrose that increases rapidly and has fairly large purple blooms. 'Blutenkissen' (see page 53), is, as its name suggests, a cushion variety with blood-red flowers. 'Schnee kissen' ('Snow Cushion') (see page 54), with pure-white flowers, makes a fine sight as it spreads rapidly.

There are several very good white primroses; the white form of *P.* 'Wanda', called simply 'White Wanda' (see page 55), is a very prolific flowerer. 'Queen of the Whites' (see page 56) is one of the best, with shapely flowers with a yellow eye and red-tinted stems to set them off over dark glossy leaves. 'Snow White' is very similar to 'Snow Cushion' but it has rather larger flowers, whilst 'The Bride' is a charming free flowering polyanthus-primrose. A very old white form of *P. vulgaris* found in Cornwall long before the coming of *P. juliae* is 'Harbinger', which was awarded a Royal Horticultural Society first class certificate in 1886. It is now very rare, though there are 'Harbinger' seedlings about.

Some favourite primroses have been the result of serendipity, perhaps turning up in a bed of *P. juliae* seedlings. One such was a fine double, which appeared at T. Smith's garden at Daisy Hill, Newry; he named it 'Pat' after his youngest daughter, but some time later a lady wrote to tell him that she had already named a primrose 'Pat' and he therefore called his primrose 'Our Pat' (see page 57). It has been a great favourite with primrose growers ever since. Whilst it does not make very large clumps it is a most robust plant that divides and carries on extremely well. The attractive leaves are pinky-bronze when young, turning to purple-green as they age. One sees many differing descriptions of the flowers because the colour changes as the light catches them and as they age, so that a clump may give the impression of purple shot through with rich blue. T. Smith's own description written to Mrs McMurtrie is 'a *juliae* hybrid of vigorous growth with purple-tinted foliage and perfect double flowers of the most beautiful shade of sapphire shaded in certain lights to blue purple'.

Another happy find was 'Kinlough Beauty' (see page 58) which turned up in the garden of Mrs Johnson at Kinlough in Co Leitrim, again among *P. juliae* seedlings. It has striking flowers of dusky pink with a cream stripe down the centre of each petal. In the same batch of seedlings, according to Cecil Monson of Co Roscommon, was another polyanthus-primrose carrying delicate flowers of palest translucent yellow over attractive rich-green foliage; this was named 'Lady Greer' (see page 59) after the lady who lived at Cunagh Grange, Co Kildare. This flower is sometimes described as 'tinged pink', and I have seen the tips of the petals of hitherto ordinary yellow flowers take on a slight pinkish tone, but I think this is due to climate or soil, as it occurs rarely. There appears to be a 'Pink Lady Greer' (though I have not seen it) which was offered by the Margery Fish nursery several years ago. Similar to 'Lady Greer' is 'Dorothy' (see page 60), a polyanthus with pale-yellow flowers, its petals rather wavy and cleft. This was mentioned in a letter from J. M. Douglas Smith to the Rev J. McMurtrie in 1948, who lists it among other Canadian primroses he had obtained from British Columbia. Yet another pale little polyanthus-type primrose raised by Dr McWatt is 'McWatt's Cream' with small cream flowers, along with 'McWatt's Claret' (see page 61), a very compact polyanthus with light-coloured claret flowers.

A primrose of very delicate colouring is 'Iris Mainwaring' (see page 62), a neat little plant with small, pinky-lilac flowers over good deep-green foliage, ideal for rockeries and 'nooks and crannies' with a pocket of good soil. 'Beamish Foam' (see page 63) is a charming and very floriferous primrose with many little blooms of pale yellow flushed with pink held well above the foliage. Genders lists a 'Pink Foam' in his nursery catalogue as well as 'Beamish Foam' which he describes as 'similar in all respects to Pink Foam except that its pale-pink flowers are flushed with yellow'. The Glazely catalogue for 1965 lists 'Beamish Pink Foam', describing the plant as 'very pale pink flowers produced, sometimes, on polyanthus stems, and continues, 'our stock is guaranteed to be true, as our original plant came from Beamish where the first plant occurred as an accidental seedling'. A froth of 'Beamish Foam' together with the deep blue *Myosotis* is a pretty sight.

The 'pansy primrose' 'Romeo' (see page 64) is one of my favourites. It has a flattish face of a lovely violet colour, is a strong grower and blooms obligingly early. It looks well planted with the dwarf varieties of narcissus, such as 'Tête-a-Tête' or 'Baby Moon', as does the primrose 'Blue Riband' (see page 65) raised in Scotland by George Murray. This plant has a flamboyant flower, quite a good bloom with a bright-red edge to the eye – it blooms early and long, and is a vigorous grower.

There is a fine variety of red Juliana primroses to choose from, and most of them are good, vigorous growers. One of the best, raised by E. B. Champernowne at Buckland Monachorum in Devon, is 'David Green' (see page 66), which is of a rich red. There seems to be some difference of opinion about this flower; Hecker calls it eyeless and Genders describes it as having 'an almost complete lack of eye', whilst Champernowne himself, described it as having a 'striking golden eye' and Townsend as 'with a striking eye'. I have had plants from two impeccable sources and both have a little gold eye as in the illustration. 'Cherry' is another cheerful red – an old variety of rather trim and compact habit. 'Gloria' is of a darker red, more a bright crimson, and is one of the first juliana hybrids. Genders describes it as having white markings on the inside of the petals, whilst Townsend writes of a 'distinct white vein' on the petal; on my plant some flowers have this and some not. In 1965 Champernowne introduced 'Buckland Wine' (see page 67), one of the finest of the red hybrids; its flowers glow like a beacon on a sunny spring morning, over rich dark crumpled foliage. About the same time, in 1966, Cecil Monson of Co Roscommon, Eire, raised a fine red with a touch of cerise in it, which he named 'Dr Molly' (see page 68), after Dr Molly Sanderson who has a fine garden at Ballymoney. A polyanthus-primrose of a rather similar cerise red is 'Lingwood Beauty' (see page 69), but some of the petals are slightly cut at the edges, giving an attractive appearance.

The light-green leaves are a good foil for the flowers. The old pre-*juliae* primrose 'Miss Massey' is now very rare indeed. It was mentioned in *Popular Garden Flowers*, by Walter Wright (published in 1911), and is still in existence; it is a little compact plant with rich-red flowers over fresh bright-green foliage.

A plant of a very different shade of red is the little 'Tomato Red' (see page 70) given to me several years ago by the Lady Anne Palmer who created a beautiful garden at Rosemoor in Devon. It was given to her by 'Cherry' Collingwood Ingram, though she is not sure whether he actually raised it. This cheerful little primrose was originally sent out with the name 'Tomato' but sometime later when it went for trials to the Royal Horticultural Society it was pointed out that one cannot name one plant after another, hence the change to 'Tomato Red'. Collingwood Ingram did, however, raise the splendid primroses 'Ingram's Red' and the richly coloured 'Ingram's Blue' (see page 71), which I also have from the Lady Anne, together with another unusual blue from Devon, 'Zeal Denim' raised at Zeal Monachorum – a blue with no hint of purple.

The person who has had the greatest influence upon our primroses in more recent times is Florence Bellis, of Gresham, Oregon, USA. This intrepid lady, seeking a home during the harrowing depression of the 1930s, settled in a rather derelict barn which became her home and a haven of peace. To eke out a living she grew and sold plants and in 1934 ordered some polyanthus and primrose seed from Sutton's catalogue for a few precious dollars. At that time the polyanthus was creating a lot of interest among growers, and nurseries on both sides of the Atlantic were concentrating on producing new colours and strains, among them Suttons in England and Frank Reinelt in California.

Florence Bellis, self taught, and with only the most primitive of equipment, not only successfully grew on her polyanthus plants but embarked upon a programme of hand pollination which was to result in some of the most beautiful polyanthus ever produced, in pure colours hitherto unknown. She issued her first Barnhaven list in 1939.

The Primroses

About 1946 when everybody seemed to be producing larger and brighter polyanthus, a stir was caused by Blackmore & Langdon's 'Gold Medal' strain and also by Reinelt's 'Pacific' strain – though, to my eyes, these flashy flowers had none of the gentle quality of the Barnhaven strains. Another lady from Oregon, Linda Eickman, gave Florence Bellis some pink-flowered plants, from which came the 'New Pinks'. Linda Eickman was given the highest award from the American Primrose Society in 1953.

In the sixties Florence Bellis decided to retire and sent her collection of polyanthus and single and double primroses in a wealth of colours and forms to England, where it has flourished ever since under the care of Jared and Sylvia Sinclair and their expert team in Cumbria.

The Sinclairs have produced a wide variety of polyanthus in the 'Silver Dollar' strains, some examples of which are 'Paris 90' (see page 72), in creams and blues with a picotee edge, 'Striped Victorian' with petals veined in different colours and 'Chartreuse', in shades of cream tinted lime green. Many of these flowers seem to have a marked rose-eye at the throat. This occasional feature of primroses was well described by Miss G. Jekyll VMH, when addressing the Royal Horticultural Society's primula conference on Wednesday April 16, 1913. She referred to a 'raised, fretted ridge at the edge of the tube forming a kind of crown and giving the flower what is called a rose-eye'.

The Sinclairs have distributed seed right across the world, from their polyanthus strains and single primroses and their enchanting doubles. There must be many like myself who have used their seed and the resulting double flowers to raise other colours over the years. My best, 'Lucy Murray', was raised in 1977 and is still flourishing. It is a rich crimson with a silvery edging to the petals and is an extremely prolific flowerer, over a long period.

There is to be another change in the Barnhaven story as the Sinclairs themselves are now retiring. However, the collection is to be carried on; in future its new home will be in Brittany.

Many Barnhaven double primroses have been reproduced through micropropagation over the last few years. Some of the most striking are 'Miss Indigo' (see page 73), an almost navy-blue double frosted with white; 'Lillian Harvey' (see page 74), a later flowering, deep rose pink, very floriferous and tough; 'Eugenie' (see page 75), one of my favourites, having petals of a good blue flushed rose at the base, making quite a striking show; 'Corporal Baxter', a fine dark velvety crimson; 'Val Horncastle' and 'Marianne Davy', a good pale yellow and cream. 'Sunshine Susie' (see page 78) is a little too garish for me, as is 'Ken Dearman' (page 77), a mixture of gold shot with orange. I prefer 'Alan Robb', which is a delicate pale apricot.

Some of the most recent double primroses are the Hopley's varieties. Sixty-five plants were obtained from a small nursery near Invercargill in the South Island of New Zealand in 1979, having been originally bred there, probably from Barnhaven seed. Hopley's suffered severe losses in the terrible winter of 1981-2, as a great number of their plants were in pots – a lesson here for us all to over-winter in the ground. However, by 1984 they were able to offer forty-three different primroses. I have had 'Rhapsody' (see page 79) since 1984 and, though not a robust grower, it flowers well for me. 'Ladybird' (see page 80), also offered in 1984, is very showy, though the stems seem to have difficulty holding up the large fully double flowers.

And so, the fascinating primrose story continues, with new varieties being produced and old ones being rediscovered, giving endless pleasure to those willing to seek them out and give them loving care.

CHAPTER 4

GROWING PRIMROSES

Primroses play a most important role in my garden in spring time and early summer. Drifts of our native *P. vernales* under the still bare trees, with little Tenby daffodils, and a few late *Cyclamen coum* make the very picture of spring; and clumps and cushions of the many coloured Juliana hybrids, give a foretaste of the bright summer flowers to come. A little later, cowslips, *P. veris*, and oxlips, *P. elatior*, put in an appearance in a quiet corner where they have the chalky conditions that they like. These have married with other primroses to produce quite a variety of colours and sizes.

Primroses in general are not difficult plants, although some of the doubles and old varieties can be more demanding and unpredictable. Over the past twenty-five years or so I have discussed the cultivation of primroses with many leading primrose growers and have tried out their various theories under my own garden conditions. This has been a fascinating exercise, leading to the realisation that whilst working along the lines best suited to local conditions of soil and climate it is also important to be open to new ideas. Thus, in setting out guidelines for the successful cultivation of primroses I must stress that this is what works for me, growing primroses at a height of about 300ft (100m) in the North of England, on very slightly acid loam.

When choosing the best site for primroses, first consider how the wild ones grow. It is frequently stated that primroses are plants of the woodland floor but this gives a very misleading impression of their needs. Although they grow at the edge of woodland and in clearings, they do not thrive in deep woodland shade, and those plants that do grow there will not readily flower. In primrose country they can be seen in great drifts on sunny slopes in open fields, on railway embankments and studding the sunny sides of deep lanes, all enjoying the gentle spring sunshine. Later, when flowering is over and the plants are building themselves up again the verdure grows up around them until they are quite engulfed in a cool damp shade giving them protection from the hot summer sun and drying winds. There is no need to grow garden primroses in a mass of weeds, and certainly the doubles would be most unhappy in such off-hand conditions, nevertheless a lesson is there. The great authority on primroses and polyanthus, Thomas Hogg, who worked at Paddington Green early in the nineteenth century, said that primroses required a position 'exposed to the morning rays of the sun and excluded from them for the rest of the day'. Gardeners without trees can take heart, for shrubs and low walls will give admirable shelter from the midday sun and drying winds. Failing that, the owner of even the smallest area can provide protection for his primroses by planting a few herbaceous perennials, which will grow up and give shelter during the summer months.

For those with large numbers of primroses it may be convenient to move them to shaded sites after flowering. A simple construction covered with shade netting will be ideal, provided it is high enough to allow the plants to keep cool and airy at all times. Close, airless conditions encourage fungal diseases.

Because primroses like to be kept moist at all times it does not mean that they like to have their roots in water constantly – waterlogged soil means lack of oxygen round the roots and the plants will drown – adequate drainage is of the utmost importance. Considering primroses flourishing on embankments, slopes and hedgerows, from which excess water soon drains one acknowledges the wisdom of Major G. H. Taylor who said that the best place for growing primroses was a shady bank. Sometimes it is said that primroses thrive on heavy clay. This idea is quite mistaken; primroses require soil that never dries out in summer but at other times is well drained, and not waterlogged. Untreated clay soon sets concrete hard in dry summers and in winter it remains cold, wet and clammy, so those with heavy clay will need to improve the texture and drainage with the addition of peat, leaf mould and weathered ashes or grit, together with anything that will encourage humus and worms, like mushroom or garden compost, the contents of old grow-bags and manure. Where primroses do grow naturally on soil of a clay nature, it will have been constantly mulched and enriched with decaying fallen leaves. In sandy soil, which is very free draining, the nutrients tend to leach out rapidly and there is also a risk of rapid drying out. Conditions will be greatly improved by the addition of humus in the form of well rotted manure, compost or spent hops.

Primroses will grow satisfactorily in any good soil, but the ideal conditions for growing old varieties and doubles is a well dug bed of good loam, neutral to slightly acid, with some old rotted manure well worked into the top 12in (30cm), together with good leaf mould or peat. This gives a rich, friable tilth where worms will be encouraged to aerate the soil, and where the plants will have plenty of nutrition and a cool, moist, root run. If using peat, or, preferably, one of the excellent peat substitutes now available, it is as well to ensure that it is thoroughly damp before incorporating it into the soil. When incorporating materials such as sand or sharp grit to encourage drainage, it should be very well distributed and worked into the soil. If allowed to form pockets these would remain cold and lacking in nutrition and would prove inhospitable to the searching roots of the plants.

To grow well established primroses in pots use the same good mixture as they would have in the prepared ground, always bearing in mind that it is essential that they have a cool root run. This means long-tom pots, with the usual drainage. Clay pots are preferable but deep plastic pots will do, as long as they allow plenty of room for the roots. They should always be plunged into frames or beds, and never be left standing on top of the ground where they would warm up in summer and freeze in winter. Pots must not be allowed to dry out, so pay special attention to their watering.

Whilst primroses seem happiest grown in the ground, it is pleasant to lift a few plants in early February, bring them into the cool greenhouse and thence to a windowsill indoors – provided that they are kept cool and moist at all times. It is best to stand the potted primrose on a dish or tray of damp grit or sand, to provide a moist environment. A little damp moss around the base of the plant helps to keep the soil from drying too rapidly. One or two plants of 'Barrowby Gem' (if you are lucky enough to possess it) will scent a room, while the bright little Juliana hybrids or gold-laced polyanthus will cheer up the dark days of later winter. The plants should not be allowed to get too warm, and should be returned to the greenhouse within ten days or a fortnight, and thence outside again when the weather allows.

The time for planting primroses varies somewhat in accordance with soil and weather conditions. They are good-natured plants and do not seem to resent lifting and planting out at any time. Of course, most plants ordered from nurseries come in pots anyway or, if lifted from the open ground, a good nurseryman will always see to it that they have a nice ball of soil on the roots and that this is kept moist and held together firmly during transit, so there is really very little stress to the plant. However do not plant when the ground is freezing hard, nor during hot, dry, summer weather. I favour early autumn – about October, when the ground is still warm enough for the new incumbent to settle in and put down a few roots before the winter sets in – or spring when the ground is beginning to warm up and conditions are encouraging.

Give the plants a good soaking for half an hour before planting, and then see that the planting hole is large and, particularly, deep enough to take the spread-out roots. Primroses, like most plants, do not like their roots curled round and round to enable them to sit in whatever size hole the gardener has in mind for them – it is better, if necessary, to trim a little from the ends of long roots. If the plants have been potted for some time it may be necessary to disentangle carefully the roots and then spread them out in their new position. They must be planted deep enough to ensure that the soil comes right up around their necks, to give essential nourishment to the very top roots, then the ground must be gently firmed around them. After this water well and, if necessary, give extra protection against drying spring winds or early hard frosts in winter. Bear in mind if you cover the plants, there must be plenty of ventilation for air to circulate, or they may fall prey to botrytis.

Few plants flower over such a long period and so prolifically as the primrose. Apart from a few out-of-season flowers, a few blossoms can confidently be expected in very early spring (if the weather is kind), and certainly 'Barrowby Gem' will be glinting in the winter sunshine, and scenting the air all around if it is at all warm. Others will soon follow. The showy 'Blue Riband' always seems to flower early for me, and, together with the early glowing red 'Gloria' and 'Queen of the Whites', the flowers make a cheerful sight.

Sometimes people ask about the advisability of letting plants flower in the autumn and winter in case this should jeopardise the show of flowers in spring and early summer. In the past I have removed these buds, but for some time now I have left them to open, taking off the flowers for welcome winter posies, and have found no lessening of flowers on these plants later on. However, do remove some of the flowers on precious double primroses if they are being over exuberant in their normal flowering. You need to harden your heart to remove blooms from a magnificent cushion of over 120 flowers, but these are best restricted to about eighty blooms – or in some cases less so as not to debilitate the plant. Dead heading is always carried out, unless saving seed, in which case the plants are marked and watched.

Following flowering, the plants are given a 'thank you' feed of manure water. After soaking the manure in a container of water it must be diluted before applying. Many years ago I enquired of a well known gardener what was the correct strength and was told that traditionally it should be 'the colour of good ale'. This has been my guide ever since. For years I have not used inorganic fertilisers on my primroses, most particularly the doubles. The late Dick Taylor told me that his father, Major H. C. Taylor, of Glazeley Primroses, lost a catastrophic number of double primrose plants when they were inadvertently sprayed with fertiliser (not by him, I hasten to add) and I have certainly killed off plants with Growmore in planned experiments. However Phostrogen is used from time to time on young plants and those modern primroses which have evolved in a rather different environment from the old ones.

After flowering the primrose starts to build itself up again, put out new roots, and probably produce new crowns, so this is when it needs nourishment. Great attention must be paid also to the neck of plants, just under the leaves, for this is where it will put out those new roots. I make my own 'special mixture', given below, which is infinitely preferable to simply mulching with rotted manure forked over the surface.

Half fill an old zinc bath or a metal wheelbarrow with very well rotted manure – free of all weeds. Onto this put an equal quantity of just-damp peat, or peat substitute, and crumbly leaf mould. Then, don a pair of rubber gloves and rub the one into the other, as if rubbing fat into flour to make pastry. This takes a little time, but it is not in the least unpleasant; you can sit at the job, and really well rotted manure has the texture of Christmas cake, and is almost odourless. This mixture is then spread around the plants, pushing it under the leaves and around the neck of each plant. This is a far kinder way to apply a manure mulch than spreading in the ordinary way; roots soon find their way into the finer, crumbly mixture and slugs are not harboured as they would be under larger pieces, which tend to dry out on top and get pushed about by foraging birds and thus exclude light and air. This mulch is laid to a depth of about 2in (5cm), and not only feeds the plants but keeps the ground moist; it will also for the most part suppress weeds, while any that do arise can be picked out with no trouble. After this give one or two feeds of weak manure water, but beware of over feeding which may result in soft pampered plants whose flowers will have etiolated floppy stems unfit to hold up the blooms.

Primroses need a little consideration to their winter needs too. A good leaf mould or peat mulch in autumn gives protection and will also assist those plants that are raised up by the frosts. This is a very real winter hazard so regular inspection is necessary. Any plants with necks and roots above soil level should be firmed in and top dressed, pushing the mulch under the leaves as after flowering, or they will perish through exposure and lack of nourishment. Primroses do not mind freezing conditions and cold winter winds, but do not care for prolonged wet of the cold clammy sort. For this reason tunnel protection is a good idea for the more treasured plants, though the need for plenty of ventilation is paramount at all times, even in the coldest weather.

Dividing Primroses

By now the plants, well fed and kept watered and shaded from strong sunlight, will have built themselves up again and in many cases will be ready for division. There seems to be some confusion among less experienced primrose growers as to when to divide plants, and indeed the reason for doing so. Primroses and polyanthus of the *P. vulgaris* type have a central root stock, often called the 'carrot' from which the fibrous roots spread out and from which new crowns are formed around the parent plant. In time the old root stock becomes woody and useless and may even begin to rot, and this can spread throughout the plant. Another reason for dividing is that a plant that becomes crowded with crowns will get insufficient nourishment to sustain it all; crowns can get 'crowded out' and be pushed up out of the soil where they will find no sustenance. There is a general rule that division should be done every two years, but it's better to be guided by the plant – some vigorous growers increase so fast that yearly division does not come amiss, whilst others may not be ready for three years.

The *juliae* type primroses have a different root system and many of them spread very rapidly by creeping root stocks or rhizomes. As these form new crowns they may be severed from the parent plant without disturbing it – useful in the case of especially precious plants. The cushion-forming *juliaes* tend to make a great mound of pushed up rhizomes about the centre and these must be separated and planted out or, if not too tightly thrust together, simply covered with rich soil and left to grow through.

There is no absolutely hard and fast rule about the correct time to divide primroses, it is a matter for individual gardeners to consider what is best suited to their own conditions. Some like to split up their plants immediately after flowering, others do so in autumn, while those living in very favoured locations are able to divide twice a year, although this is not to be recommended as a general rule. This task is best carried out when the plants have had long enough after flowering to build themselves up, while still being early enough for the newly planted offsets to get their roots down and form new growth before the autumn comes and the soil cools down. This means it is usually done in mid-summer, at the end of July or early August. In a hot dry summer this may have to be delayed until autumn for it would be folly to divide plants in drought conditions.

When dividing primroses it helps to take several large, clean, empty flower pots, plenty of labels and a marking pen. Each plant can then be put into a separate pot together with its label, thus making sure that there are no muddles, and all end up correctly named. At the potting bench each plant has its roots carefully shaken free of soil over a tray, not onto the working surface, so that any pests will be contained in the tray and will not infest the other plants. Be particularly on the look-out for vine weevil grubs and aphids. All root stock must be examined for any rot and if present, it must be cleanly removed, and the cut surface dusted with flowers of sulphur – unless of course it is to be discarded anyway. Check also for any spent fibrous roots, which will present themselves as flat and light brown in colour instead of the usual round shape and cream colour. This done dip all the roots in a solution of Hexyl, or other insecticide plus fungicide, shaking off all excess.

They can then be divided, preferably by pulling new crowns away from the old root stock. Sometimes it is necessary to use a knife, in which case it should be sterilised in methylated spirit between plants to avoid carrying any infection from one plant to another. (An old rule of primrose growers stated that one should never take a knife to a polyanthus and, although there is no scientific reason for this, I still 'pull a polyanthus' in case they really did know what they were talking about.) Dust all cut or torn surfaces with flowers of sulphur and either replant in a prepared bed, or if desired, pot up in long-toms. The roots must not be curled around during this process – trim long roots back to about 4in (10cm). Twist off the leaves of large plants, leaving only about 3in (7.5cm) behind so that the newly divided plant does not have to support superfluous foliage, but don't do this to small plants with few leaves nor to small *juliae* type plants, as there would be insufficient foliage left to see the plant through. Keep the newly planted labelled divisions shaded and well watered, and lightly spray them over in the morning and evening.

If the plant is very precious you will be anxious to preserve every piece, so if the old rootstock looks healthy and not too woody it is worthwhile giving it a chance to grow on. This 'carrot' should be planted in a deep pot with its trimmed-off top level with the top of the soil. Cover the pot with a Perspex dome and put into a cool shady place. I have successfully grown new plants from many old rootstocks in this way, severing the new plantlets as soon as they have made sufficient roots to sustain themselves.

Raising from Seed

Primroses may also, of course, be raised from seed. If this is to be saved from your own plants, take great care to harvest it at just the right time. Once the seed capsules have fattened up and are beginning to brown inspect them daily, as they can very easily split and cast their contents upon the ground before you can gather them. Harvesting is usually in mid-summer and seed should be sown fresh for the best results. Seed which cannot be sown straight away, together with bought seed, should be stored in an airtight container in the bottom of the refrigerator and sown early the following spring. Sow the seed in a tray of John Innes seed compost which has been well soaked and drained and which has a thin covering of sharp sand or fine grit; this helps to keep the compost moist and to deter the growth of algae and liverwort. Do not cover the seed, simply place a sheet of glass over the tray to preserve humidity. Make sure air circulates freely all round the tray by standing it on four small bricks (a child's building bricks are just right for this job). Put the trays in a light and airy place away from direct sunshine. It is essential that the compost is never allowed to dry out – stand the tray in water when necessary to ensure a thorough watering rather than spraying over the top.

The seeds will germinate in three or four weeks. When large enough to handle they are pricked off into deep boxes containing drainage at the bottom and a growing-on compost, such as John Innes No 2 or Levingtons. If using the latter, scatter grit over the top between the plants, again to discourage algae. If sown in summer, the grown-on plants are ready to pot up and put into the frame or line out in a tunnel by mid-late autumn, where they will have protection in the winter but remain cool and airy. After pricking off seedlings, stand all seed trays and the remaining compost in the 'seed pan cemetery' – you may be rewarded by finding seedlings that have germinated many months later. This is especially useful when sowing doubles, as often the best ones are the last to germinate.

Hybridising

A lot of pleasure and sense of achievement may be gained from raising your own hybrids. It is not difficult or complicated – my nine-year-old grandson has hybridised with great success and minimal supervision. It consists of dusting pollen from the anthers of one primrose onto the stigma of another. Although all single flowers have both stamens and stigma, in the pin-eyed flower the stigma arises above the stamens up to the throat, and in the thrum-eyed the stamens are at the top whilst the stigma is much further down (see page 17). It is possible to cross thrum with thrum, and pin with pin but nature really intends a thrum x pin cross and, as a microscope will show, the stigma of the pin-eyed flower is faceted in a certain way and the thrum pollen grains are shaped to fit these surfaces, so, although it is possible to cross thrum with thrum or pin with pin, a more successful result will ensue from the correct pin x thrum cross.

Having chosen the parent plants, it is convenient to pot up the seed-bearing plant, and catch the flower to be pollinated as it is about to open, thus ensuring that insects haven't been there first. Cut away the petals and stamens very carefully, taking care not to get pollen on the stigma. Either remove the stamens from the other parent with tweezers or use a fine sable brush to dust the pollen onto the stigma. Cover the plant with a muslin cap or a plastic dome for a week to prevent insect interference, and record the cross.

Raising double primroses is rather a different matter and requires perseverence, for it could take several generations of selected crossings to produce any double flowers at all. The doubling characteristics are recessive and will always be dominated by the single. In general, double flowers replace their reproductive organs with petals so where should you start? While this is so in most doubles, some do produce anthers, sometimes only in later-blooming flowers. These pollen-producing doubles include 'Prince Silverwings', 'Our Pat', 'Paddy' and 'Marie Crousse', and pollen from these may be taken in the usual way to fertilise the selected single primrose.

In recent years another means of producing new plants has been developed – this is micropropagation where minute particles of shoot tips of a selected plant are raised in culture media under sterile laboratory conditions, producing very healthy and vigorous plants.

Pests and Diseases

Given first class growing conditions and attention to plant hygiene, on the whole primroses are trouble-free plants.

Slugs can be a nuisance, but these can be kept under control by the use of slug pellets. Take the trouble, though, to go around each day and remove the bodies, to safeguard birds and hedgehogs. Slug tape is also very effective.

Birds that vandalise the flowers constitute the most common problem. There is no real solution, apart from growing great numbers of primroses. In recent years I have had no trouble and can only suppose that with so many flowers the birds feel 'outfaced'. Some people string black thread over the plants as a deterrent but I discarded this method many years ago after a blue tit became entangled in the thread. Most of the damage seems to occur early in the morning, so a large piece of netting thrown over the beds overnight can prove helpful.

Greenfly *(aphis)* do not seem to be a great problem with primroses, although if they do attack they can cause considerable damage by sucking sap from the foliage, which will turn yellow and become limp. Fortunately these can be cleared up by spraying with any of the proprietary makes of systemic insecticide.

Red Spider *(Tetranychus telarius)* can be a pest when the conditions are very hot and dry. It causes the leaves to become mottled, but the mite cannot be seen properly with the naked eye. Systemic insecticide will be helpful. Do not confuse red spider mite with the tiny scarlet spider sometimes seen scurrying over the leaves – they are quite harmless.

Vine weevils *(Oriorrhynchus sulcatus)* are the real scourge of the primrose grower, and seem to have greatly increased in recent years. The adult beetles are about ⅓in (9mm) long and are a dull, blackish colour mottled with light brown. They themselves do little serious damage to the plants, except for eating around the edges of the leaves, but they lay their eggs at the necks of the plants in early summer and the resulting larvae can destroy a healthy specimen in a very short time. The larvae are slightly curled, creamy grubs with light-brown heads. They burrow down after hatching and feed upon the roots of the plants, then they pupate in the soil. In early spring you may dig up the young weevils, looking like ghosts of their parents, with ivory-coloured bodies, legs, antennae and wing pads. Inspect all plants regularly. Any showing signs of wilting should be lifted and examined and the soil shaken out over a newspaper. Any grubs should be either killed or fed to the resident robin at once. Isolate and examine all incoming plants for these pests before planting out. I have found them on cyclamen and fuchsias in particular, but they can turn up anywhere.

Eradication of vine weevils is not easy, since the most effective control, Aldrin, is now prohibited, but thorough soaking with HCH or Permethrin made up to spraying strength can prove useful. I also favour Bromophos or Hexyl. Dusting around the necks of the plants with naphthalene in the form of crushed mothballs deters egg laying.

Chlorosis is a yellowing of the leaves and can be caused by waterlogged soil conditions or mineral deficiencies. In the former case the remedy lies in improving the drainage, and in the latter giving trace elements in the form of Multitonic will be beneficial, though it may take a little time before the plant looks really happy again.

Virus diseases that can attack primroses are little understood and complex. There is no known cure. Leaves become yellow and blotchy and growth may be stunted. If one is unlucky enough to find a plant attacked by virus it should be taken up and burned forthwith. However, it may well be a rare old beauty that is affected. In this case, follow a rigorous spraying routine with systemic insecticides to prevent the disease being conveyed to other plants by insects.

Botrytis cinerea is a mould that occurs in poor light and persistent cold damp conditions. It will proliferate among dead leaves and other decaying material, so remove dying foliage and dust the scars with flowers of sulphur. Spraying with fungicide will also help prevent botrytis.

Neck rot and **Primula root rot**, caused by *Phytophthora parasitica* and *Theilaviopsis basicola*, can be a problem in very wet conditions. Cut out the affected parts as soon as possible, dust with copper lime dust, spray with fungicide and improve the drainage.

Primula wilt, also called brown core (*Phytophthora primulae*), can occur where large numbers of primroses have been grown in the same place for a very long time and the disease has built up in the soil. The only thing to do here is to move all plants to another site and do not grow them on that spot again for a number of years. Alternatively, sterilise the soil in the vacated bed with 2 per cent solution of formalin applied at the rate of 5 gal per sq yd (25l per sq m). Take great care to see that no formalin solution leaches out onto the grass or other plants as it will, of course, kill everything with which it comes into contact. Where the bed is reasonably small, dig out the soil altogether and put it in a safe place on a sheet of heavy duty polythene which has had the edges of the base turned up and stapled so that it forms a container and then soak with the formalin solution. Label the container clearly. Whichever method is used, after soaking with the formalin cover with polythene for 24 hours or so and thereafter fork the soil over from time to time. After about four weeks sow a little cress seed and if it germinates the soil is ready for use – if not give it a little longer.

Fungal diseases may account for the way apparently healthy primroses sicken and die for no obvious reason.

The possible fungal-disease link occurred to me in the summer of 1986, one grey, cold, wet day followed another, and several plants, particularly the doubles, were looking as though they were anticipating a visit from the Great Reaper. The prevailing excessive wet and cold and poor light provided ideal conditions for fungal diseases, such as *Theilaviopsis basicola*, which can get a hold on a plant without revealing any symptoms. The high nitrogen content of the soil due to routine feeding would also encourage fungal diseases, and this would be exacerbated by giving more feed or water.

I rigged up a 'polythene roof' above the plants to give some protection from the wet, while allowing plenty of air to circulate. They were given potash, about 2oz per sq yd (30g per sq m), and sprayed weekly then fortnightly with alternate doses of 'Fungus Fighter' and 'Benomyl'. Happily, all but one of these plants recovered and the treatment has been repeated since to good effect.

Of course there will be other reasons why plants should inexplicably fail, but fungal diseases should be considered.

BIBLIOGRAPHY

Blunt, W. &   *The Illustrated Herbal*
  Raphael, S.   (Weidenfeld & Nicolson, 1979)
Culpepper   *The Complete Herbal*   (1817)
Fish, M.   *Cottage Garden Flowers* (Collingridge, 1961)
Genders, R.   *Collecting Antique Plants* (Pelham Books, 1971)
      Primroses   (John Gifford, 1959)
Genders &   *Primroses & Polyanthus*
  Taylor   (Faber & Faber, 1954)
Gerard, J.   *Herball*   (1597)
Gilbert, S.   *The Florist's Vade Mecum*   (1683)
Hecker, W.R.   *Auriculas & Primroses*   (Batsford, 1971)
Hibberd, S.   *Field Flowers*   (Groombridge, 1870)
McWatt, J.   *The Primulas of Europe* (Country Life, 1923)
Nelson, E.C.   *'Irish Primroses' – Journal of the*
    American Primrose Society   (1984)
Parkinson, J.   *Paradisi in sole Paradisus*
    Terrestris   (1629)
    Theatrum Botanicum   (1640)

Rea, J.   *Flora, seu de Florum Cultura* (1665)
Routh, S. & J.   *Leonardo's Kitchen Notebook*
        (Collins, 1982)
Royal   *Primula Conference April 16th*
  Horticultural Society   (RHS, 1913)
Smith, Burrow   *Primulas of Europe & America*
  & Lowe   (Alpine Garden Society, 1984)
Smith, Sir W. &   Section *vernales Pax.*
  Fletcher, H. R.   (pages 402-468 from The
    Transactions of The Botanical
    Society of Edinburgh
      vol XXXIV part IV, 1946-7)
Smith-Wright, W. &   *The Sections of The Genus*
  Forrest, G.   *Primula* (H.M.S.O. vol. XVI
    No LXXVI Pages 1-50
    from Notes from the Royal
    Botanic Gardens Edinburgh, 1928)

ACKNOWLEDGEMENTS

My grateful thanks to all those 'Primrose Friends', with whom I have exchanged plants and information over the years; in particular Mrs Mary McMurtrie and Mr David Chalmers who unearthed, and sometimes copied out, a great deal of interesting old material and put their seal of approval on the illustrations. To Dr Molly Sanderson for useful information from Ireland, and to Pam Gossage, the Lady Anne Palmer, Ailsa Jackson, Andrew Norton and Stephen Craven, all of whom provided plants for me to paint when my own were not in flower.

To Dr Charles Nelson for information, especially on Irish primroses, and to Jared Sinclair for bringing me up to date on developments at Barnhaven.

Also to Dr Brent-Elliott at the Lindley Library, Mr John Harthan, R.K. Francis of the Art Library at the Victoria and Albert Museum, and the enterprising staff of the Library at Skipton-in-Craven, all of whom assisted my research.

My thanks also to Rosemary Asquith who valiantly turned what seemed like miles of tape into readable manuscript, to Vivienne Wells of David & Charles under whose amicable guidance producing the book became a most happy experience, and my husband who kept the household running on oiled wheels and compiled the index.

And last, but by no means least, to Geoffrey Smith, without whose enthusiasm and initial 'push' this book would not have come about.

INDEX

VARIETIES